TREASURE HUNT ACROSS AMERICA

ILLUSTRATIONS
BY CATHY MORRISON

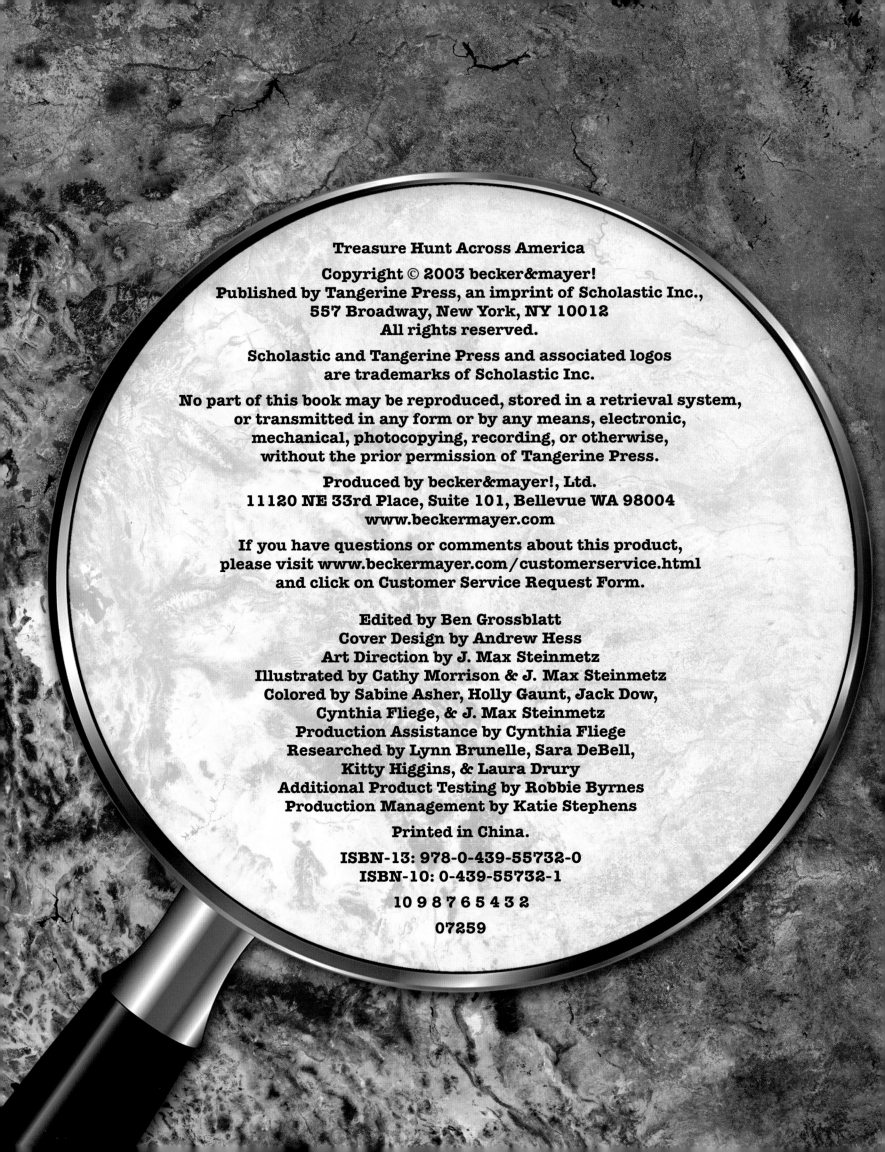

Produced by becker&mayer!, Ltd.
11120 NE 33rd Place, Suite 101, Bellevue WA 98004
www.beckermayer.com

If you have questions or comments about this product,
please visit www.beckermayer.com/customerservice.html
and click on Customer Service Request Form.

Edited by Ben Grossblatt
Cover Design by Andrew Hess
Art Direction by J. Max Steinmetz
Illustrated by Cathy Morrison & J. Max Steinmetz
Colored by Sabine Asher, Holly Gaunt, Jack Dow,
Cynthia Fliege, & J. Max Steinmetz
Production Assistance by Cynthia Fliege
Researched by Lynn Brunelle, Sara DeBell,
Kitty Higgins, & Laura Drury
Additional Product Testing by Robbie Byrnes
Production Management by Katie Stephens

Printed in China.

ISBN-13: 978-0-439-55732-0
ISBN-10: 0-439-55732-1

10 9 8 7 6 5 4 3 2

07259

TREASURE HUNT ACROSS AMERICA

① Eye-popping maps are stuffed to the borders with colorful cartoons.

② Checklists at the back of the book challenge you to find people, places, and things in each state.

③ Search the states to match the cartoons in the checklists to the pictures on the maps.

Let the Treasure Hunt begin!

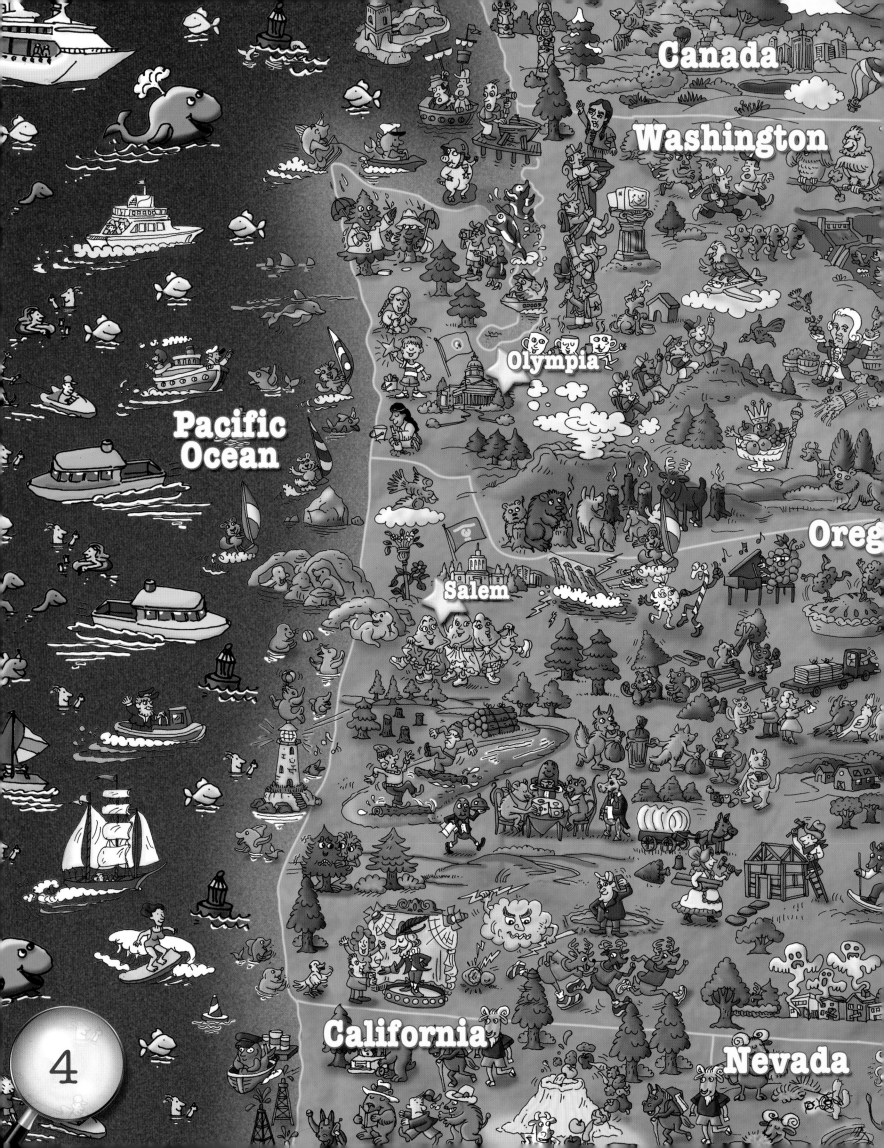

Canada

Washington

Pacific
Ocean

Olympia

Oreg

Salem

California

Nevada

4

Washington

FIND ME!

The Evergreen State • 42nd state to join the USA • 18th largest state

The Olympic Peninsula is the setting of a temperate RAINFOREST.

More APPLES are grown here than in any other state.

MOUNT RAINIER is an active volcano.

Oregon

FIND ME!

The Beaver State • 33rd state to join the USA • 9th largest state

The Columbia Gorge is a popular spot for WINDSURFERs.

PEPPERMINT is grown here.

The THREE SISTERS are mountains in the Oregon Cascades.

Idaho

FIND ME!

The Gem State • 43rd state to join the USA • 14th largest state

The volcanic soil in this state is perfect for growing POTATOes.

Agate is a GEMSTONE mined in Idaho.

The Nez Perce first bred the spotted APPALOOSA horse hundreds of years ago.

Full checklists begin on page 27

Montana

Idaho

Boise

Utah

Wyoming

California
The Golden State • 31st state to join the USA • 3rd largest state

The San Andreas Fault is the scene of many EARTHQUAKEs.

LIGHTS! Camera! Action! Hollywood is the movie-making capital of the nation.

Gilroy is known as the GARLIC capital of the world.

Nevada
The Silver State • 36th state to join the USA • 7th largest state

Nevada has an official state fossil: the ICHTHYOSAUR.

The Pershing County COURTHOUSE is the only round courthouse in the country.

Many people have claimed to see UFOs and aliens here.

Utah
The Beehive State • 45th state to join the USA • 13th largest state

PRAIRIE DOGs recognize group members by kissing them.

The inventor of the TELEVISION was born here in 1906.

The Vernal BANK was built from bricks sent through the mail.

Arizona
The Grand Canyon State • 48th state to join the USA • 6th largest state

PETRIFIED WOOD comes from Arizona's Petrified Forest.

Arizona is known as the "Nation's VALENTINE" because it joined the union on February 14.

The RINGTAIL is the state's official mammal.

FIND ME!

6

Full checklists begin on page 27

Idaho

Utah

Wyoming

Colorado

Salt Lake City

Arizona

New Mexico

Phoenix

Mexico

7

Canada

Montana

Idaho

Helena

Wyoming

Colorado

Che...

FIND ME!

Montana

The Treasure State • 41st state to join the USA • 4th largest state

FLATHEAD LAKE is the largest natural freshwater lake in the West.

Grasshopper Glacier contains GRASSHOPPERs that got trapped in the ice.

Dinosaur EGGS have been discovered at Egg Mountain.

Wyoming

The Equality State • 44th state to join the USA • 10th largest state

This was the first state to demand wrapped BREAD.

Since 1937, one of the world's largest STEAM ENGINEs has been in Holiday Park.

Wyoming was the first state where women had the right to VOTE.

Canada

Minnesota

North Dakota

Bismarck

South Dakota

Pierre

Iowa

North Dakota

The Flickertail State • 39th state to join the USA • 19th largest state

Turtle Lake is known for its TURTLE races.

Dickinson's DINOSAUR museum houses full-scale specimens.

The world's largest BUFFALO monument is in Jamestown.

South Dakota

The Mount Rushmore State • 40th state to join the USA • 17th largest state

The city of Clark stages a MASHED POTATO wrestling contest.

The RING-NECKED PHEASANT is the state bird.

The Mitchell CORN PALACE is covered with corn.

9

Full checklists begin on page 27

Colorado

The Centennial State • 38th state to join the USA • 8th largest state

A wooden CAROUSEL in Burlington is the oldest in the country.

A CAR on the road from Idaho Springs to Mt. Evans is driving on the highest paved road in North America.

The STREETs of Victor are paved with low-grade gold.

New Mexico

The Land of Enchantment • 47th state to join the USA • 5th largest state

Deming is known for its DUCK RACEs.

In Lake Valley, the silver was so pure it could be sawed off in BLOCKs.

Hatch is the GREEN CHILI capital of the world.

Full checklists begin on page 27

FIND ME!

FIND ME!

Colorado

Denver

Arizona

Santa Fe

New Mexico

Nebraska

Kansas

Topeka

Missouri

Texas

Oklahoma City

Oklahoma

Arkans

Lou

Kansas

FIND ME!

The Sunflower State • 34th state to join the USA • 15th largest state

During a HAILSTORM in Coffeyville, a 2-pound hailstone fell.

AMELIA EARHART was the first woman to fly solo across the ocean.

Kansas State U. specializes in veterinary medicine for HORSEs.

Oklahoma

FIND ME!

The Sooner State • 46th state to join the USA • 20th largest state

Every July, Terral holds a WATERMELON festival.

The world's biggest PECAN PIE was baked in Okmulgee.

The state amphibian is the BULLFROG.

Minnesota

Canada

North Dakota

Wisconsin

South Dakota

St. Paul

Iowa

Des Moines

Illin

12

Minnesota

The Gopher State • 32nd state to join the USA • 12th largest state

RED PINES are a state symbol.

Paul Bunyan and his blue OX Babe are characters in American folklore.

The common LOON is the state bird.

Wisconsin

The Badger State • 30th state to join the USA • 23rd largest state

People came from around the world to see the WHITE BUFFALO, a symbol of peace.

Bloomer is the JUMP ROPE capital of the world.

The first KINDERGARTEN in the country opened here.

Michigan

The Wolverine State • 26th state to join the USA • 11th largest state

Michigan is the only state with a floating POST OFFICE.

The nation's first SODA POP (ginger ale) was developed here.

Detroit is known as MOTOR City.

Full checklists begin on page 27

FIND ME!

FIND ME!

FIND ME!

Santa Fe

Texas

Oklahoma City

New Mexico

Mexico

Texas

The Lone Star State • 28th state to join the USA • 2nd largest state

In 1992, road workers here found a 9,000-year-old SKELETON.

JACKRABBITs can be found across the state.

The Adopt-a-HIGHWAY program began here in 1985.

FIND ME!

Arkansas

The Natural State • 25th state to join the USA • 29th largest state

The only active DIAMOND mine in the country is near Murfreesboro.

COSMIC CAVERN is one of Arkansas's many caves.

Arkansas is home to an ELEPHANT and wildlife sanctuary.

FIND ME!

Oklahoma

Arkansas

Tennessee

Mississippi

Little Rock

Alaba

Jackson

Louisiana

Baton Rouge

Austin

Louisiana

The Pelican State • 18th state to join the USA • 31st largest state

LOUIS ARMSTRONG, a pioneer of jazz, was born in New Orleans.

The state dog, the CATAHOULA LEOPARD DOG, has webbed feet.

People use FLATBOATS to travel in the bayous.

FIND ME!

Mississippi

The Magnolia State • 20th state to join the USA • 32nd largest state

The TEDDY BEAR was inspired by an actual event that took place here.

Vardaman is the SWEET POTATO capital of the world.

The BOTTLE-NOSED DOLPHIN is the state's marine mammal.

FIND ME!

Full checklists begin on page 27

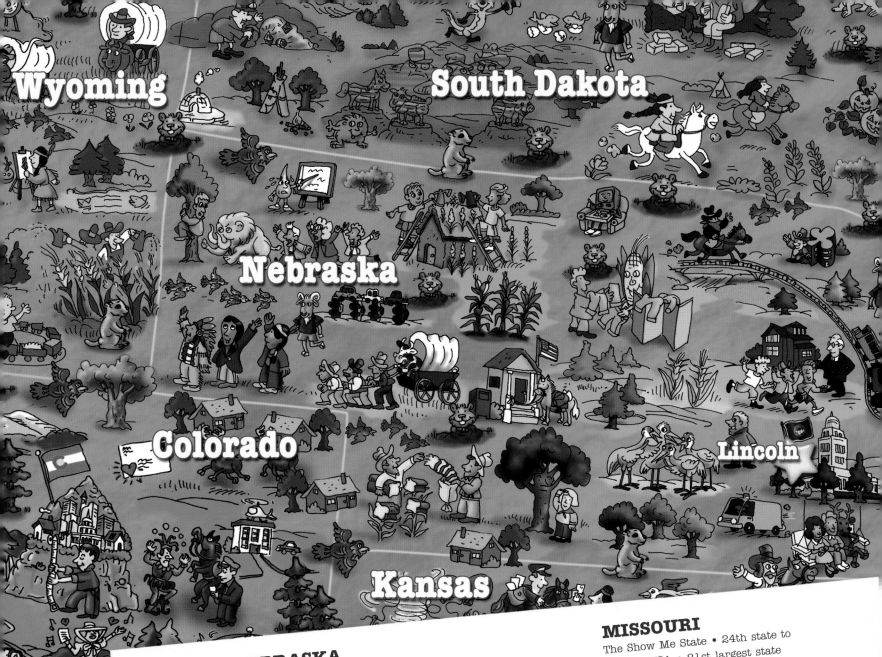

Wyoming

South Dakota

Nebraska

Colorado

Lincoln

Kansas

New Mexico

NEBRASKA
The Cornhusker State • 37th state to join the USA • 16th largest state

FIND ME!

The 911 EMERGENCY system started here.

Arbor Day, the day to honor TREEs, was founded by a Nebraskan.

MAMMOTH fossils have been found here.

IOWA
The Hawkeye State • 29th state to join the USA • 26th largest state

FIND ME!

The world's most crooked street, sometimes called SNAKE Alley, is in Burlington.

STEAMBOATs used to travel up and down the Mississippi.

The state rock of Iowa is the GEODE.

MISSOURI
The Show Me State • 24th state to join the USA • 21st largest state

FIND ME!

The first successful PARACHUTE jump from a plane was in St. Louis, in 1912.

Missouri was the setting for adventure books by MARK TWAIN.

Next to Rome, Kansas City has more FOUNTAINs than any city in the world.

ILLINOIS
The Prairie State • 21st state to join the USA • 25th largest state

FIND ME!

Chicago's famous deep dish PIZZA was introduced in 1943.

The tallest man ever was born in Alton, in 1918. He was 8' 11" and wore a size 37 SHOE.

ABE LINCOLN is buried in Springfield.

Full checklists begin on page 27

Texas

Oklahoma

Minnesota

Wisconsin

Michigan

Iowa

Des Moines

Illinois

Missouri

Springfield

Topeka

Jefferson City

Kentucky

17

Arkansas

New York

The Empire State • 11th state to join the USA • 27th largest state

The first PIZZA restaurant opened here in 1895.

The Baseball HALL OF FAME is in Cooperstown.

Troy is the birthplace of the UNCLE SAM symbol.

Vermont

The Green Mountain State 14th state to join the USA 45th largest state

A SEA MONSTER named Champ is said to live in Lake Champlain.

SUGAR MAPLE TREEs, the source of maple syrup, grow here.

In 1834 SANDPAPER was developed by a Springfield inventor.

Massachusetts

The Bay State • 6th state to join the USA • 44th largest state

Springfield is the site of the BASKETBALL Hall of Fame.

The nation's first SUBWAY line opened in Boston, in 1897.

CRANBERRY bogs are located on Cape Cod.

Connecticut

The Constitution State • 5th state to join the USA • 48th largest state

In 1775, American colonists published the country's first NEWSPAPER here.

Eli Whitney, inventor of the cotton gin, was one of the first to build a FACTORY for mass production.

Ella Grasso was elected the country's first woman GOVERNOR, in 1974.

Maine

The Pine Tree State • 23rd state to join the USA • 39th largest state

The coat of a Maine COON CAT is well-suited to the harsh climate.

The CHICKADEE is Maine's state bird.

PAPER is one of the state's leading products.

New Hampshire

The Granite State • 9th state to join the USA • 46th largest state

People report BLACK BEAR sightings in this state.

SNOWSHOES are a great way to get around in snowy, mountainous terrain.

New Hampshire has over 1300 lakes and PONDS.

Rhode Island

The Ocean State • 13th state to join the USA • The smallest state

The oldest SCHOOLHOUSE in the country was built here in 1716.

Newport is the scene of a yearly JAZZ festival.

JEWELRY is a major industry here.

Full checklists begin on page 27

Canada

Maine

Vermont

Augusta

Montpelier

New Hampshire

Concord

Boston

Massachusetts

lbany

Hartford

Rhode Island
Providence

Connecticut

ey

Indiana

The Hoosier State • 19th state to join the USA • 38th largest state

Johnny Appleseed roamed the Indiana frontier in the early 1800s, planting APPLE trees as he went.

The first professional BASEBALL PLAYERs played here.

The Little 500 is Bloomington's annual BIKE RACE.

Kentucky

The Bluegrass State • 15th state to join the USA • 37th largest state

Middlesboro is the only American city built within a meteor CRATER.

The Peace BELL rings in Newport.

Kentucky BLUEGRASS is called that for the blue flowers that bloom in it each May.

Ohio

The Buckeye State • 17th state to join the USA • 34th largest state

Cleveland is home to the ROCK 'N' ROLL Hall of Fame.

The BUCKEYE of the state's nickname is actually a horse chestnut tree.

Akron is the RUBBER capital of the world.

West Virginia

The Mountain State • 35th state to join the USA • 41st largest state

The first MOTHER'S DAY was observed in Grafton.

The AUTOHARP is an instrument used in bluegrass music.

The world's largest SYCAMORE tree grows in Webster Springs.

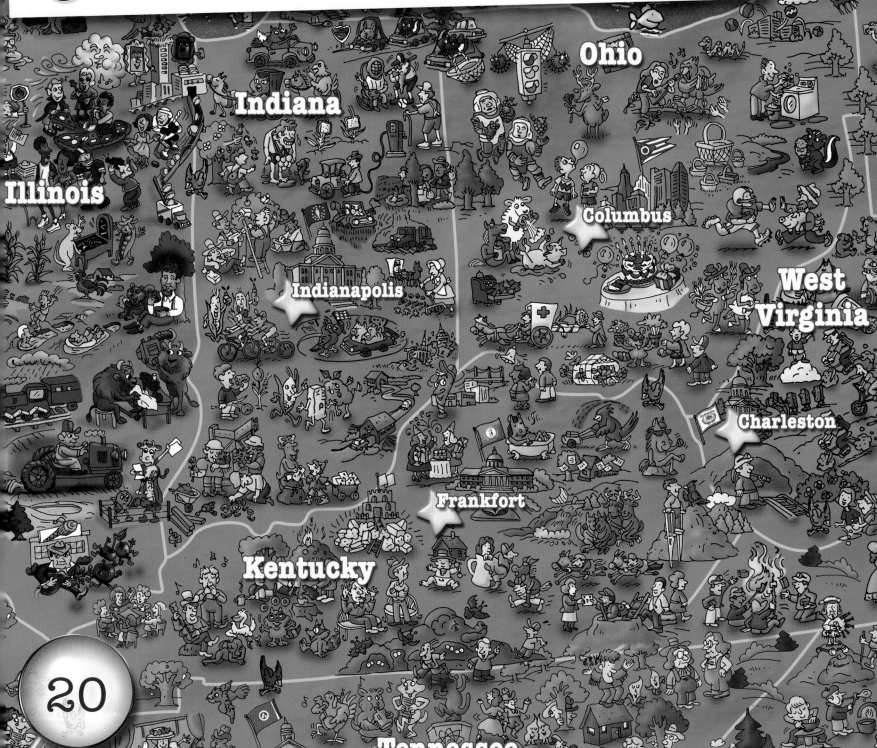

Massachusetts

New York

Albany

Pennsylvania

New Jersey

Harrisburg

Trenton

Maryland

Annapolis

Dover

Virginia

Delaware

Richmond

Washington, D.C.

Raleigh

Lake Ontario

North Carolina

Pennsylvania

The Keystone State • 2nd state to join the USA • 33rd largest state

Ben Franklin wanted the TURKEY, and not the bald eagle, for the national symbol.

Philadelphia is home to the LIBERTY BELL.

Betsy Ross made the first American FLAG here.

New Jersey

The Garden State • 3rd state to join the USA • 47th largest state

The Atlantic City BOARDWALK is popular with tourists.

New Jersey is sometimes called the nation's MEDICINE CHEST.

One of the world's tallest WATER TOWERs can be found here.

Maryland

The Old Line State • 7th state to join the USA • 42nd largest state

The first school to teach dentists how to fix TEETH was here.

EGRETS live in Havre de Grace.

BLACK-EYED SUSANS are the state flower.

Delaware

The First State • 1st state to join the USA • 49th largest state

The constellation Ursa Major has a STAR named Delaware Diamond.

Some of America's first LOG CABINs were built here

Delaware's state bird is the BLUE HEN CHICKEN.

Virginia

Old Dominion • 10th state to join the USA • 35th largest state

Assateague Island has been the home of wild PONIES for centuries.

SOLDIERS fought more than half of the Civil War's battles here.

This state is home to the world's only museum of OYSTERS.

21

Full checklists begin on page 27

Kentucky

Tennessee

Nashville

Georgia

Mississippi

Alabama

Atlanta

Montgomery

Jackson

Florida

Tallahassee

Virginia

North Carolina

Raleigh

Columbia

South Carolina

Tennessee
The Volunteer State • 16th state to join the USA • 36th largest state

Miners in this state dig up the copper to make PENNIES.

Tennessee has the nation's largest UNDERGROUND LAKE.

The Tennessee WALKING HORSE is a breed that originated here.

Alabama
The Yellowhammer State • 22nd state to join the USA • 30th largest state

The town of Enterprise built the BOLL WEEVIL MONUMENT.

The Talladega SPEEDWAY is the world's biggest motorsports facility.

The TUSKEGEE AIRMEN made history during World War II.

Georgia
The Peach State • 4th state to join the USA • 24th largest state

Boiled PEANUTs are a favorite Georgia snack.

Okefenokee Swamp is home to the American ALLIGATOR.

Dahlonega was the scene of the country's first GOLD rush.

North Carolina
The Tar Heel State • 12th state to join the USA • 28th largest state

The VENUS FLYTRAP is found only within 100 miles of Wilmington.

Duplin Country is home to the world's biggest FRYING PAN.

The nation's tallest LIGHT-HOUSE is at Cape Hatteras.

South Carolina
The Palmetto State • 8th state to join the USA • 40th largest state

The CAROLINA WREN eats insects and spiders.

BARRACUDA live in South Carolina's waters.

The yellow JESSAMINE FLOWER looks like a trumpet.

23

Full checklists begin on page 27

Georgia

Florida

Tallahassee

Florida

The Sunshine State • 27th state
to join the USA • 22nd largest state

The endangered MANATEE needs
water that is 68° F or warmer.

An AIRBOAT is a popular way
to travel in the Everglades.

RACE CARS compete at
Daytona Beach.

FIND ME!

Full checklists
begin on page 27

25

Alaska

The Last Frontier • 49th state to join the USA • The largest state

One way people travel over snowy terrain is by DOG SLED.

Scientists believe a land bridge to Alaska led many a Siberian HUNTER to the New World.

In the middle of summer, the SUN never sets in Barrow.

Hawaii

The Aloha State • 50th state to join the USA • 43rd largest state

Waxing the top of your SURFBOARD keeps your feet from slipping.

MONGOOSES were brought to Hawaii to take care of a rat problem.

The Hawaiian Island chain was formed by VOLCANOes.

Full checklists begin on page 27

Alabama p.22

- ☐ MONTGOMERY is the capital city.
- ☐ DR. MARTIN LUTHER KING, JR. led the Freedom March from Selma to Montgomery in 1965.
- ☐ HELEN KELLER, inspiring author and social crusader, was born here.
- ☐ The YELLOWHAMMER, the state bird, is a kind of woodpecker.
- ☐ George Washington Carver developed hundreds of new uses for the PEANUT.
- ☐ CAMELLIA flowers are used to make tea.
- ☐ Saturn ROCKETs and other spacecraft were developed in Huntsville.

Alaska p.26

- ☐ JUNEAU is the capital city.
- ☐ Woolly MAMMOTH fossils have been found in Alaska's ice and frozen ground.
- ☐ The tallest PEAK in North America, Mt. McKinley, is also called Denali.
- ☐ ICEBERGs break off of Alaska's estimated 100,000 glaciers.
- ☐ The Alaska PIPELINE carries oil from Prudhoe Bay to Valdez.
- ☐ Tongass National FOREST is found here.
- ☐ There are twice as many CARIBOU here as people.

Arizona p.7

- ☐ The capital city is PHOENIX.
- ☐ Arizona has more species of HUMMINGBIRDS than any other state.
- ☐ At one time, CAMELs were used to move goods and supplies across Arizona.
- ☐ KAIBAB SQUIRRELs are found only on the Kaibab Plateau.
- ☐ Arizona is the nation's top producer of COPPER.
- ☐ KACHINA DOLLS are special to the Hopi.
- ☐ More TELESCOPEs can be found in Tucson than anywhere else in the world.

Arkansas p.15

- ☐ The capital city is LITTLE ROCK.
- ☐ Mt. SEQUOYAH is named after the Cherokee scholar who developed a writing system for the Cherokee language.
- ☐ The "living museum" at the Ozark Folk Center keeps the traditional skills of the quilter and BLACK-SMITH alive.
- ☐ The state rock, bauxite, is used to make ALUMINUM.
- ☐ Former president BILL CLINTON was born in Hope.
- ☐ Different varieties of RICE are grown here.
- ☐ The highest point in the state is MAGAZINE MOUNTAIN.

California p. 6

- ☐ SACRAMENTO is the capital city.
- ☐ The color of the GOLDEN GATE BRIDGE is officially known as International Orange.
- ☐ More AVOCADOs are grown here than in any other state.
- ☐ The world's tallest tree is a REDWOOD in Montgomery Woods State Reserve (it's 367.5 feet tall).
- ☐ Los Angeles has the worst TRAFFIC in the country.
- ☐ Many people are working to restore the CONDOR population.
- ☐ Southern California is known for its SURFER culture.

Colorado p.10

- ☐ The capital city is DENVER.
- ☐ Tourists visiting MESA VERDE can see the homes of ancient cliff dwellers.
- ☐ Katharine Lee Bates wrote "AMERICA THE BEAUTIFUL" after being inspired by the view from Pikes Peak.
- ☐ Hundreds of thousands of VALENTINEs pass through the Loveland post office every year.

- ☐ DOVE CREEK is the pinto bean capital of the world.
- ☐ The biggest silver NUGGET ever found in North America was dug up near Aspen in 1894. It weighed close to a ton!
- ☐ The ocean and wind created the landscape of Great SAND DUNES National Monument more than a million years ago.

Connecticut p.19

- ☐ HARTFORD is the capital city.
- ☐ Tourists can charter a BOAT for deep-sea fishing.
- ☐ OYSTERS are gathered on the coast.
- ☐ SAILBOATers enjoy the state's 250 miles of coastline.
- ☐ Harriet Beecher Stowe, the author of the influential novel "Uncle Tom's CABIN," lived and died here.
- ☐ SUBMARINEs are built here.
- ☐ Hartford is known for its INSURANCE companies.

Delaware p.21

- ☐ DOVER is the capital city.
- ☐ This state was the NUMBER ONE state to ratify the Constitution.
- ☐ SOYBEANS are an important crop.
- ☐ Delaware Bay is home to more HORSESHOE CRABs than any other place in the world.
- ☐ Factories here supplied soldiers with GUNPOWDER.
- ☐ The American HOLLY is the state tree.
- ☐ Great blue HERONs live here.

Florida p.24

- [ ] TALLAHASSEE is the state capital.
- [ ] ORANGES are a major crop.
- [ ] HURRICANEs can do a lot of damage.
- [ ] Miami boasts distinctive Art Deco BUILDINGs.
- [ ] The SPACE SHUTTLE is launched from Cape Canaveral.
- [ ] In the 1500s, Ponce de Leon searched for the FOUNTAIN of youth.
- [ ] Key LIME pie is named for fruit that grows in the Florida Keys.

Georgia p.22

- [ ] ATLANTA is the capital city.
- [ ] Former president JIMMY CARTER was a farmer here.
- [ ] The state is famous for its PEACHes.
- [ ] Baseball greats HANK AARON and TY COBB are associated with Georgia.
- [ ] The 20-foot-tall Peanut MONUMENT is in Ashburn.
- [ ] Atlanta is one of the country's fastest-growing METRO AREAs.
- [ ] The TEXTILE industry is important here.

Hawaii p.26

- [ ] HONOLULU is the capital city.
- [ ] A HULA DANCER tells a story with her hands while moving to music.
- [ ] PINEAPPLEs are a major crop.
- [ ] PEARL HARBOR is a United States naval base on the island of Oahu.
- [ ] The state's official flower is the HIBISCUS.
- [ ] Mount Waialeale on the island of Kauai is one of the wettest places on Earth.
- [ ] The LEI, or flower necklace, is given as a sign of friendship.

Idaho p.5

- [ ] The capital city is BOISE.
- [ ] Hells Canyon is the deepest GORGE in the country.
- [ ] CRATERs of the Moon National Monument is a tourist attraction.
- [ ] The state bird is the MOUNTAIN BLUEBIRD.
- [ ] The SAWtooth Mountains are found here.
- [ ] BALANCED ROCK is one of Idaho's spectacular natural attractions.
- [ ] One of the state's important crops is SUGAR BEETS.

Illinois p.17

- [ ] SPRINGFIELD is the capital city.
- [ ] The SEARS TOWER is the tallest building in the US.
- [ ] Chicago is known as the PINBALL capital of the world.
- [ ] The ice cream SUNDAE was named in Evanston.
- [ ] The two major crops are soybeans and CORN.
- [ ] The country's largest archaeological site is at the Cahokia MOUNDS.
- [ ] A revolutionary PLOW that could cut right through hard prairie ground was developed in Illinois.

Indiana p.20

- [ ] INDIANAPOLIS is the capital city.
- [ ] Many attend the Indianapolis 500 to cheer on their favorite RACE CAR.
- [ ] STEEL WORKERS are part of one of the state's biggest industries.
- [ ] For its size, Indiana has more interstate HIGHWAY miles than any other state.
- [ ] Fort Wayne was the setting for the first practical GAS PUMP.
- [ ] Levi and Katie Coffin of Fountain City ran a busy "STATION" on the Underground Railroad.
- [ ] Parke County is the COVERED BRIDGE capital of the world.

Iowa p.17

- [ ] DES MOINES is the capital city.
- [ ] FARMs cover much of Iowa.
- [ ] The WILD ROSE is the state flower.
- [ ] Animal-shaped MOUNDS can be seen at Effigy Mounds National Monument.
- [ ] Iowa's state tree is the OAK.
- [ ] Iowa State University is headquarters for science RESEARCHERs.
- [ ] Former president HERBERT HOOVER was born here.

Kansas p.11

- [ ] TOPEKA is the capital.
- [ ] A primitive HELICOPTER was invented here in 1909.
- [ ] Kansas boasts the richest SALT deposits in the world.
- [ ] Kansas is known for its big SUNFLOWERs.
- [ ] In the Wizard of Oz, a TORNADO carries Dorothy's house away from Kansas.
- [ ] A PONY EXPRESS RIDER carried mail across Kansas to San Francisco in 1860.
- [ ] The state is sometimes called America's BREAD BASKET.

Kentucky p.20

- [ ] FRANKFORT is the capital.
- [ ] MAMMOTH Cave is the largest mapped cave system in the world.
- [ ] "HAPPY BIRTHDAY to You" was written by two Louisville sisters in 1893.
- [ ] Joe Bowen walked on STILTS from Kentucky to California.
- [ ] A big chunk of the country's gold reserves are kept at FORT KNOX. (The door to the vault weighs more than 20 tons.)
- [ ] The Kentucky Derby is an important race for people who like RACE HORSEs.
- [ ] Paducah is the site of a big QUILT museum.

Louisiana p.15

- [ ] BATON ROUGE is the capital city.
- [ ] FORTUNE TELLERs and other mystics delight visitors in New Orleans.
- [ ] The BROWN PELICAN is the state bird.
- [ ] Thomas Jefferson bought the territory of Louisiana (and other states) from NAPOLEON in 1803.
- [ ] The PIRATE John Lafitte is said to have buried treasure in the swamps here.
- [ ] Because it was such a profitable crop, cotton was known as KING Cotton.
- [ ] The state tree is the BALD CYPRESS.

Maine p.19

- [ ] AUGUSTA is the capital city.
- [ ] The LIGHTHOUSE beacon guides ships.
- [ ] BLUEBERRIES are grown and harvested here.
- [ ] LOBSTER fishing is a major industry in this state.
- [ ] Ninety percent of the nation's wooden TOOTHPICKS are made in Maine.
- [ ] Mt. Katahdin is the first MOUNTAIN in the country to see the sunrise.
- [ ] No county in the country has more acres devoted to POTATO cultivation than Aroostook County.

Maryland p.21

- [ ] ANNAPOLIS is the state capital.
- [ ] The attack on FORT McHENRY was Francis Scott Key's inspiration for "The Star Spangled Banner."
- [ ] CLARA BARTON, whose home was in Glen Echo, founded the Red Cross.
- [ ] The GODDARD SPACE FLIGHT CENTER in Greenbelt is the site of important space research.
- [ ] When JOUSTERs do their thing in Maryland, they're participating in the state sport.
- [ ] In 1784, a 13-year-old boy went airborne in the country's first successful piloted BALLOON launch.
- [ ] Baltimore was home to the country's first UMBRELLA factory, in 1828.

Massachusetts p.19

- [ ] BOSTON is the state capital.
- [ ] During his famous Midnight Ride, PAUL REVERE warned colonists the British were about to invade.
- [ ] Pilgrims on the Mayflower landed at PLYMOUTH ROCK in 1620.
- [ ] A man in Rockport made an entire HOUSE out of rolled-up newspapers. (He worked on the house for 20 years!)
- [ ] Salem was the scene of the infamous WITCH trials of the 1690s.
- [ ] Native Americans and Pilgrims enjoyed the first THANKSGIVING here.
- [ ] The BOSTON TEA PARTY rebellion was in 1773.

Michigan p.12

- [ ] LANSING is the capital city.
- [ ] Battle Creek is called the world's CEREAL BOWL.
- [ ] One of Michigan's nicknames is the WOLVERINE State.
- [ ] The main breeding sites of the rare KIRTLAND'S WARBLER are in Northern Michigan.
- [ ] Holland, Michigan is famous for its Dutch theme, including WINDMILLs.
- [ ] The DWARF LAKE IRIS is the official state wildflower.
- [ ] FREIGHTERs on Michigan lakes can be more than 1,000 feet long.

Minnesota p.12

- [ ] The capital city is ST. PAUL.
- [ ] The first open-HEART surgery was performed at the University of Minnesota.
- [ ] There are more than two hundred MUD LAKEs in Minnesota.
- [ ] LAURA INGALLS WILDER (author of the "Little House" books) lived on the banks of Plum Creek.
- [ ] 1,200 miles of SNOWMOBILE trails criss-cross Brainerd.
- [ ] A Minnesota invention: the pop-up TOASTER (it came along in 1926).
- [ ] Duluth is the busiest inland PORT in the country.

Mississippi p.15

- [ ] JACKSON is the capital.
- [ ] The Petrified FOREST, near Flora, is home to trees that are 30 million years old.
- [ ] The Pascagoula River is known as the SINGING RIVER because of the "singing" sound it makes.
- [ ] COTTON is a major crop here.
- [ ] The state flower is the MAGNOLIA.
- [ ] Vicksburg used to be on a BLUFF overlooking the Mississippi River, until the river's course changed in 1876.
- [ ] The state's waters are home to CATFISH.

Missouri p.17

- [ ] The capital is JEFFERSON CITY.
- [ ] The ICE CREAM CONE was invented at the 1904 St. Louis World's Fair.
- [ ] Missouri's state animal is the MULE.
- [ ] It took him 50 years, but a man here grew a BEARD that was twelve and a half feet long.
- [ ] The state was named after the Missouri Indians, and their name meant "CANOE-havers."
- [ ] The GATEWAY ARCH in St. Louis was completed in the mid-1960s.
- [ ] The state tree is the flowering DOGWOOD.

Montana p.8

- [ ] The state capital is HELENA.
- [ ] The BITTERROOT is the state's flower.
- [ ] The nation's largest herd of roaming ELK is found here.
- [ ] Outside of Alaska, Montana has the largest GRIZZLY BEAR population in thecountry.
- [ ] Many people here get electricity from power made by a DAM.
- [ ] Montana is home to the largest breeding population of TRUMPETER SWANS in the lower 48 states.
- [ ] The Yogo SAPPHIRE is the only gem from North America included in England's crown jewels.

Nebraska p.16

- [ ] LINCOLN is the capital.
- [ ] In the 1800s, a pioneer family would have moved west in a COVERED WAGON.
- [ ] The largest TRAIN ROBBERY on the Union Pacific line happened here, in 1877.
- [ ] A University of Nebraska graduate revolutionized supper-time with his invention of the TV DINNER.
- [ ] Only a few PONY EXPRESS STATIONs are still around, and two are located in Gothenburg.
- [ ] The state flower is the GOLDENROD.
- [ ] Some parts of the state hold CORNHUSKING contests.

Nevada p.6

- [ ] CARSON CITY is the state capital.
- [ ] The BIGHORN is the official state mammal.
- [ ] Many towns built by SILVER miners over a century ago are still standing today.
- [ ] The state produces a lot of HAY.
- [ ] The state is in a geo-graphical area known as the Great BASIN.
- [ ] Pyramid Lake is famous for its CUI-UI fish.
- [ ] STEAM ENGINEs brought food and sup-plies to workers in the gold mines.

New Hampshire p.19

- [ ] CONCORD is the capital.
- [ ] The PURPLE LILAC, which grows on a bush in the spring, is the state flower.
- [ ] The strongest WIND ever recorded in the country (231 mph) blew on top of Mount Washington.
- [ ] This state is known for its antique TEXTILEs.

- [ ] The state bird is the PURPLE FINCH.
- [ ] The OLD MAN of the Mountain is a natural formation in Franconia Notch State Park.
- [ ] The Library of Congress, in Washington, DC, is made from New Hampshire GRANITE.

New Jersey p.21

- [ ] The capital city is TRENTON.
- [ ] In 1858, modern pale-ontology began with the discovery of a HADROSAURUS skeleton in Haddonfield.
- [ ] THOMAS EDISON built better telephone in his Menlo Park lab in
- [ ] Samuel Morse, inventor of Morse code, installed the first electric TELEGRAPH, near Morristown.
- [ ] BLUEBERRIES grow wild here.
- [ ] The state flower is the VIOLET.
- [ ] Cape May is the oldest seashore RESORT in the country.

New Mexico p.10

- [ ] SANTA FE is the capital city.
- [ ] The ROADRUNNER, New Mexico's state bird, can run 15 mph!
- [ ] SCIENTISTs at Los Alamos Scientific Laboratory conduct experiments.
- [ ] Las Cruces is home to the world's largest ENCHILADA.
- [ ] Experimental ROCKETs were introduced in 1930 (now the aero-space industry is important to the state).
- [ ] Albuquerque is famous for its BALLOON festival.
- [ ] New Mexico has more sheep and CATTLE than people.

New York p.18

- [ ] ALBANY is the capital city.
- [ ] The STATUE OF LIBERTY still welcomes people to America.
- [ ] New York City FIRE-FIGHTERS protect more than 8 million people.
- [ ] The ERIE CANAL was built to help New York become a center for worldwide trade.
- [ ] The state flower is the ROSE.
- [ ] Niagara Falls is a very popular HONEYMOON spot.
- [ ] One of the marble outside the New York City Public Library is named Patience.

North Carolina

- [ ] RALEIGH is the state capital.
- [ ] The Wright Brothers made the first AIR-PLANE flight here.
- [ ] Fayetteville is the site of the country's first MINIATURE GOLF course.
- [ ] Grandfather Mountain the setting for a yearly SCOTTISH festival.
- [ ] North Carolina has more than 78,000 miles of PAVED ROAD.
- [ ] The state bird is the CARDINAL.
- [ ] TOBACCO is the main crop.

North Dakota p.9

- [ ] BISMARCK is the capital.
- [ ] More DUCKS breed in the state's wetlands than anywhere else in the country.
- [ ] SACAGAWEA, a Shoshone Native American woman, helped Lewis and Clark on their expedition.
- [ ] A stone CAIRN in Rugby marks the geographical center of North America.
- [ ] The FLICKERTAIL SQUIRREL flicks its tail before entering its burrow.
- [ ] The International PEACE GARDEN is located on the border with Manitoba, Canada.
- [ ] It's against the law to pick the WILD PRAIRIE ROSE, the state flower.

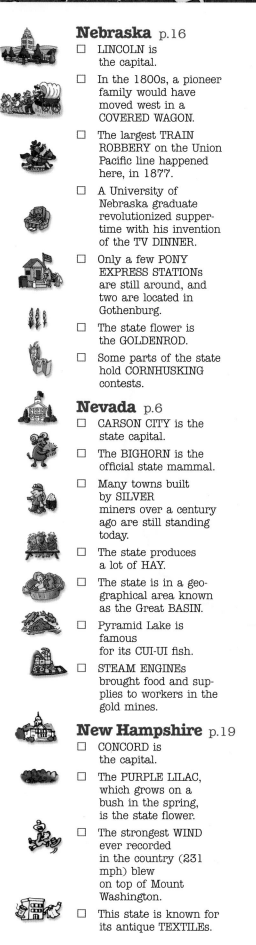

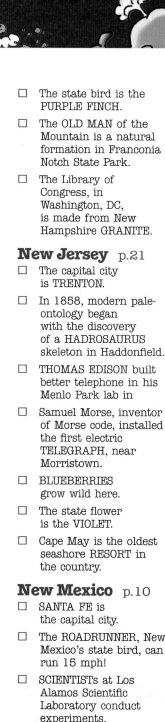
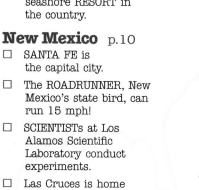

Ohio p.20

- [ ] COLUMBUS is the capital city.
- [ ] Astronauts Neil Armstrong and JOHN GLENN were born here.
- [ ] The modern TRAFFIC LIGHT was invented here.
- [ ] This state sees lots of presidential BIRTHDAYs. (Eight presidents were born here.)
- [ ] Native Americans built more than 10,000 mounds here, including SERPENT Mound in Hillsboro.
- [ ] Ohio is the country's top producer of GREENHOUSE plants.
- [ ] The first patent-holder for CHEWING GUM lived in Mount Vernon.

Oklahoma p.11

- [ ] The capital is OKLAHOMA CITY.
- [ ] The first PARKING METER was installed in Oklahoma City, in 1935.
- [ ] Oklahoma has more ARTIFICIAL LAKEs than any other state.
- [ ] The SCISSOR-TAILED FLYCATCHER is the state bird.
- [ ] The Harmon County Historical Museum features exhibits to honor the American PIONEER.
- [ ] This state is home to the National COWBOY Hall of Fame.
- [ ] WHEAT is an important crop.

Oregon p.4

- [ ] SALEM is the capital city.
- [ ] According to legend, BIGFOOT lurks on the coast.
- [ ] They used to say the soil in the Willamette Valley was so fertile you could plant a BROOMSTICK there and it would grow.
- [ ] The Columbia Plateau is made of layers of LAVA.
- [ ] The THUNDEREGG is the state rock.
- [ ] At 1,932 feet deep, CRATER Lake is the deepest lake in the country.
- [ ] Oregon produces a lot of the country's PLYWOOD.

Pennsylvania p.21

- [ ] HARRISBURG is the capital city.
- [ ] Punxsutawney Phil is the guest of honor at GROUNDHOG Day ceremonies.
- [ ] LITTLE LEAGUE BASEBALL's first World Series was held in Williamsport.
- [ ] Kennett Square is the MUSHROOM capital of the world.
- [ ] Many GUITARS are manufactured in Nazareth.
- [ ] Pennsylvania is home to the country's largest MONEY-making mint.
- [ ] BLACK CHERRIES are grown in the Borough of Kane.

Rhode Island p.19

- [ ] PROVIDENCE is the state capital.
- [ ] In a topiary garden near Portsmouth, more than 80 trees are cut into ANIMAL SHAPES.
- [ ] A famous PORTRAIT of George Washington was painted by Rhode Islander Gilbert Stuart.
- [ ] The VIOLET is the state flower.
- [ ] BLOCK ISLAND is a vacation paradise.
- [ ] The state bird is the RHODE ISLAND RED.
- [ ] Bristol hosts the longest-running series of FOURTH OF JULY celebrations in the country.

South Carolina p.22

- [ ] The capital city is COLUMBIA.
- [ ] Francis Marion, who escaped capture during the Revolutionary War, was known as the Swamp FOX.
- [ ] Colonists won a battle of the Revolutionary War in a fort made of PALMETTO logs.
- [ ] A GOLFER will find many courses to play here.
- [ ] SPANISH MOSS hangs from trees.
- [ ] One of the state's major industries is TEXTILES.
- [ ] The first shots of the Civil War were fired on FORT SUMTER.

South Dakota p.9

- [ ] PIERRE is the capital city.
- [ ] The town of Lead is the setting for the largest underground GOLD MINE.
- [ ] MOUNT RUSHMORE features the faces of four great presidents.
- [ ] The BLACK HILLS are home to Native Americans of the Great Sioux Nation.
- [ ] Sturgis hosts the annual Black Hills Classic MOTORCYCLE Rally.
- [ ] The BLACK-FOOTED FERRET has been reintroduced into the Sage Creek Wilderness Area.
- [ ] Flaming FOUNTAIN is fed by natural gas.

Tennessee p.22

- [ ] NASHVILLE is the capital.
- [ ] Frontiersman DAVY CROCKETT was born near Limestone Creek, in 1786.
- [ ] The American Museum of Science and ENERGY is in Oak Ridge.
- [ ] The MOCKINGBIRD is the state bird.
- [ ] This state is home to big AUTOMOBILE factories.
- [ ] The GRAND OLE OPRY is a popular spot for Country & Western music fans.
- [ ] During the Great Depression, the Tennessee Valley Authority built many hydroelectric DAMs.

Texas p.14

- [ ] The capital city is AUSTIN.
- [ ] The ARMADILLO is covered with bony plates for protection.
- [ ] Tyler is the ROSE capital of America.
- [ ] The RIO GRANDE RIVER is 1,960 miles long.
- [ ] In 1836, American soldiers defended THE ALAMO against the Mexican army.
- [ ] The state insect is the monarch BUTTERFLY.
- [ ] The name of the state comes from a Caddo Native American word meaning "HELLO, FRIEND."

Utah p.7

- [ ] The capital is SALT LAKE CITY.
- [ ] The Bonneville Salt Flats, the largest flat area on Earth, are used for AUTO RACING.
- [ ] At 290 feet high, RAINBOW BRIDGE is the largest natural stone bridge in the world.
- [ ] SKIERs love Utah—they say it has the best powder.
- [ ] Levan—"NAVEL" backward—is called that because it's in the center of the state.
- [ ] The first railway across the country was completed in Promontory when the GOLDEN SPIKE was pounded in.
- [ ] The state is known as the BEEHIVE State because bees symbolize Utah's hardworking residents.

Vermont p.19

- [ ] MONTPELIER is the capital city.
- [ ] Every year, the National ROTTEN SNEAKER Championship is held here.
- [ ] The first POSTAGE STAMP was made in Brattleboro.
- [ ] The first dentist to use LAUGHING GAS lived in White River Junction.
- [ ] The state's name comes from the French for "GREEN MOUNTAIN," a reference to the forested hills that run the length of the state.
- [ ] The HERMIT THRUSH is the state bird.
- [ ] Some say the RED CLOVER grown here can be used as a medicine.

Virginia p.20

- [ ] RICHMOND is the capital.
- [ ] THE PENTAGON, headquarters of the United States Department of Defense, is in Arlington.
- [ ] Founding Father and Virginian THOMAS JEFFERSON wrote the Declaration of Independence.
- [ ] BLACKSMITHing and other traditional crafts are practiced in Colonial Williamsburg.
- [ ] Virginians used the CANNON to fight the Revolutionary War.
- [ ] The state dog is the AMERICAN FOXHOUND.
- [ ] The first permanent English settlement in North America was at JAMESTOWN.

Washington p.4

- [ ] OLYMPIA is the capital city.
- [ ] Seattle is named after CHIEF SEALTH of the Duwamish.
- [ ] Many people in the Puget Sound area work in the COMPUTER field.
- [ ] The state is nicknamed The Evergreen State for its huge TREES.
- [ ] A boundary dispute between America and England in the 1800s came to a head in The PIG War.
- [ ] The AMERICAN GOLDFINCH is the state bird.
- [ ] SALMON migrate upriver.

West Virginia p.20

- [ ] The capital city is CHARLESTON.
- [ ] The state produces more glass MARBLES than any other state.
- [ ] The state's original name was Kanawha, a Native American word meaning "place of WHITE STONE."
- [ ] The CARDINAL is the state bird.
- [ ] COAL, mined here, supplies energy.
- [ ] Summers Street was the first BRICK street in the world.
- [ ] Golden Delicious APPLES originated here.

Wisconsin p.12

- [ ] MADISON is the capital city.
- [ ] Wisconsin's American Birkebeiner is the largest CROSS-COUNTRY SKIING race in the country.
- [ ] Somerset is famous for its INNER TUBES.
- [ ] GINSENG is grown here.
- [ ] Monroe is known as the SWISS CHEESE capital of the world.
- [ ] The first workable TYPEWRITER was made in Milwaukee, in 1867.
- [ ] More than twelve thousand rivers and STREAMs flow though Wisconsin.

Wyoming p.8

- [ ] CHEYENNE is the capital city.
- [ ] The bucking bronco on the state's license plates was named Ol' STEAMBOAT.
- [ ] In terms of its human population, Wyoming is the most EMPTY state in the nation.
- [ ] The SNAKE River flows through Grand Teton National Park.
- [ ] The INDIAN PAINTBRUSH isn't a paintbrush at all—it's the state flower.
- [ ] DEVIL'S TOWER was the first national monument.
- [ ] MINERs working in the Black Thunder coal mine produce two tons of coal per second!